Verdant

Jeffery Beam

Verdant

kin press

First Kin Press edition

Originally published as *Don't Forget Love* Dispatches Virtual Chapbook #3. Now revised and expanded. Dispatches Virtual Chap Books were a fragmentary sublapidary of Dispatches Editions which was a filiated figment of *Dispatches from the Poetry Wars'* promiscuous and undisciplined imagination of being together in the work of the poem. The author thanks the editors Kent Johnson and Michael Boughn, and contributing editor Steven Manuel, for their original confidence in this work. The Dispatches interactive website is now digitally archived by the Digital Library Services and Special Collections at the Simon Fraser University Library, British Columbia, Canada.

Excerpt from *Love, Again* by Doris Lessing. Copyright ©1996 by Doris Lessing. Used by permission of HarperCollins Publishers.

Giacomo Leopardi, "The Infinite," translated by W.S. Merwin, from *Selected Translations 1948-2011.* Copyright ©2013 by W. S. Merwin. Reprinted with the permission of The Permissions Company, LLC on behalf of Copper Canyon Press, coppercanyonpress.org. Also, translation Copyright ©2015, W.S. Merwin, used by permission of The Wylie Agency (UK) Limited.

 # 13 Gitanjali (Song Offerings) and *# 96 Gitanjali (Song Offerings)* by Rabindranath Tagore, version by Coleman Barks, in *What Wants to Come Through Me Now*, Lexington, KY: Fons Vitae, ©2020. Used with permission from the author.

ISBN 978-0-9989293-4-7

Kin Press
Higganum, CT 06441
kin-press.org

Verdant

For Stanley, Gene, Richard, and Alex
For Khidr, Ganesha, and John the Baptist
For those friends and guides who helped rescue me
(you know who you are)

Don't forget love;
it will bring all the madness you need
to unfurl yourself across the universe.
—Mirabai

He's the whole dark ocean of love. And for the sake of love,
Each being shall burn its own small flame.
—Rabindranath Tagore

Longing: The Dark One's Residence in the Beloved

 # 13 Gitanjali (Song Offerings)

I HAVE NOT SUNG the song I came here to sing.
    I have spent the time stringing
    and unstringing my instrument.

The words are not right. The truth of my time
    has not been said, only this
    deep longing in my heart.

The blossom has not opened in the wind.
    I have not seen his face,
    nor heard his voice.

Only the sound of his footsteps on the dirt road
    in front of my house.

I have spread the mat on the floor,
    making a place for him to sit.

but I have not lit the lamp or asked him in.
    I have lived my life hoping for this meeting,

but it has not happened yet.

Rabindranath Tagore

He leaves in a whirlwind:

Alchemical furnace

Blackbird dust

Late summer rules the grasses

The Beloved sings Love's unrelenting seizure

Enduring burning: a kind
of perplexing bleak ecstasy

And the Dark One's residence
in the Beloved

How peaceful the porch swing on summer evenings
when heat takes on shimmering coolness

How I sit to watch and listen

Faint musics shimmy from the neighbors
Cars whizz by like carousel horses

How startling the sun sinks into the maple trees' fired leaves
Oncoming silence sweet and deafening
Perfect for remembering … and forgetting

You will return? Or will your absence
become coolness—this sweet and
deafening silence?

Evening
The woods' least light kindling the breeze
Sparrows settle in branches
Water droplets on their beaks

On my cheek one bright single tear

Such teasing cruelty in your eyes
I thought them magic
Thought them fruit to be polished

Your lashes lashing me
Black lightning in a silver storm

You told me your heart was a sieve
as if to force me into condemnations
Instead I praised your wisdom—
your brown eyes dancing—
your blue-black hair smoking up our nights

Summer welcomes me again
I walk out
            Skin crying

Neighbors watching my restless solitude

You thought you owned me
but I know now
suffering alone possesses me

We had no enemies
Even blackberries withdrew small
daggers when we kissed near them

So why these lips pained and red
from poisoned kisses

To save myself
would I ever able myself into betrayal?

A night alone on the porch swing swinging

Fireflies alight on porch railings
emphatically light-hearted like I thought those kisses

Even if they live just a summer
they light their own way within
the great lumbering night

Oh how you nooned me!
The meadow rampant with goldenrod and heal-all
Grasshoppers clicking their heels

Then the storm brutal and unforgiving

Creek bed rising out of nowhere
Bee sizzle and beetle thrum silenced

My body nowhere too
Unfortunate cursed bird
Abandoned

I will write you when I am coming
Wait for me on the porch where
I left you
Near the mimosa

I want it to be evening
The sun just dropping
I want the porch to be pleasant with
tea cups and strange flowers
and dogs snoring under the table

Out of your letter's ashes
I need no gold nor silver diet

And not till afterward
a handkerchief stolen from
the black eyes of evening

I sit among summer flowers
while autumn
hovers over the fields

You said I was I can be
a God
Oh I will be!   Am!

I am wet with morning
Needing no letters
I am handsome with wit and loneliness
Grief showers me with tenderness for myself
and that enduring longing I've written you of

Well   it's a bitter drink
It curves in me like the garden path
It hides and reveals in its turning

Do you think I will forget?   Have forgotten?
You?

Words words words!
Don't expect more than that

Your lack anointed me
I stood wretched in its wrack
Rain forgot its way through the oak leaves
Troubling its way onto the moss then stopped
It gave up to sun just dappled just broken
Then rain again

You in another city where no rain falls
My streets glistening with your stride your shadow

Stepping down into the moss I wonder
How can I live?

The pine warbler trebles
She knows something I don't
Listening   I hear her telling me
promises that won't be broken

Suddenly winter

How quickly the foxes
took to their dens

For you a candle
and an unlocked door

For me moonlight pooling under porch eaves
and the dark beguiling with

Fox wail owl weep

Longing:
                Love's treasured Kabbalah

Every day I learn something new
Remembered kisses scripting my skin

Letters unsent
I've written your name backwards to un-spell it

A kind of witchcraft

A kind of kindness: The least the
most you deserve

Winter and winter and winter
No letter warms me
No fire thaws me
No bed revives me

What sunrise warms you?
What kindling burns you?
What sleep renews you?

Winter and winter and winter again

I don't know my whole body
I don't know my mind
I know only my feet cold
The mossy path
talking in whispers the way only moving talks:

from here to there and back

Learning the ground's solace
Suddenly   I'm blushing!
Beautiful again!

Winter come and gone

In the heart
In the world

From you
One final letter

> *I don't know where I am*
> *Don't look for me*

Taste of ashes

Spring and I
glide in fragrance and color
under pollen-stained greenery's
fresh beginnings

Months of imagined letters and desiring none
Months of moon moorings
Months of dull anticipations

Why was your script so hurried so ragged?

Spring took its merry time
You should too

I am thankful
where many ferns are
How tough the black root-masses
covering stretches
pale and shaggy
leaning toward the sun without regret

How perfectly the wild poor ground
shelters cheerfulness
sodden drippings
cold mists

When I was a child
I learned how good a thing
shade is   The sound of it
The same note repeated
A secret nothing

Observing things that escape
strong long-sighted people

I longed for you as the willow longs for wind
shaking its branches willingly

You called me beggar
I begged only truth:
a garnet embedded and gleaming in pyrite stone
deeper than honesty deeper than proof

Now as garnet I no longer long
for Fool's Gold's dull shine

Perfect
Free of other's expectations even
my own

Late spring heat sprung clammy on my hands
Breath startles me

Your name that's enough I think
But enough nevers itself!

The pileated's sharp call pulses through the pines

Broken hearts littering the world
Holes in the garden
                    Holes in the heart
Grief
        wonderful gift
  As long as it's not made a habit

Forgive me for wounds I've given you:
I wanted to plant flowers in you
            not thorns

I've learned to live with tensions
A monk making love to God alone in his cell
Blaming no one not even you
Thankful for the place to burn and cool

Everyone grieves with me
Are already knitting the holes with their love
Listen!   I can hear their needles
threading and moving

You think me lonely

For the first time I know stillness' frenzy

My love knows Love's every
simplest ecstasy

So this is what this Love means

And Devotion

The coarse body transmuting
the roughest whim

Anxiety soaring into revelation

I am not your acolyte but Love's pilgrim
My beard a waterfall moistening the ground

I knew you were just His shadow
when the mountain beyond gleamed
smoky blue and
sunrise silenced the whip-poor-will

I knew you were just His shadow when
my body slimmed
becoming ripples in the pond

Oh there is nothing that does not see you
The tiniest membrane of the smallest creature feels you—

Anxious neighbors watching my walks
Cars' invented rapaciousness

Little birds
Fireflies and the bent fern

You dwell inside me now
as I always dwelt in you
Wine of my cup
Cup of my wine

I drank to quiet my sorrow
but it grew wilder all the time

Now my wine springs from life's unfiltered fountain—

Joy counts and nothing else does

I have a great secret

Living close to the storm
the forest the drought and the hail
I am a beauty

The grasses kneel with me

And with my kin the moss and willow
my kin the beasts and birds

I am weather   I am astonishing
My body sibilant and muscled
The hairs on my neck and arms stand
on end

How audible your absence
How like my glass of pure well-water
Clear   now empty

How I relish that drink

Possessing you I thirst no longer

Not a bad thing at all

Was it lust making war with bones?
Or bones not
knowing what to do
                    but doing it anyway?

I dissolve in sunlight
Your dark project becoming my own
My fruit polished by lightning and tears

Nights now spent alone are enough
A small brown bird overwhelming the lilacs—
I overwhelm the flowers as well

Happiness and

    the branch bending in the dew

Don't Forget Love:
Sacred Longing's Dark Project

I have no fear
Of thy dark project, but my heart is set
On living
　　　　　—Edna St. Vincent Millay

Put out my eye, and I can see you still
　　　　　—Rainer Maria Rilke

　　　You left and once again my soul became
　Empty and serene
　　　　　—Anna Akmahtova

This is how I would die into the love I have for
you: As pieces of cloud dissolve in sunlight.

　　　There's a strange
frenzy in my head,
of birds flying, each particle,
circulating on its own.
Is the one I love
everywhere?
　　　　　—Jelalu'ddin Rumi

Even within my first memory, as a baby nursing at my mother's breast, longing has been the one persistent passion that has inhabited my life—a companion for the journey, an enemy at the gates, a presence in the air, a taste in the dirt. Desire, craving, yearning, lusting, aching, pining, hankering, hungering ... even itching. The fourteenth-century anonymous work of Christian mysticism, *The Cloud of Unknowing*, counsels, "Your whole life must be one of longing"... "This longing love is of vital importance." What to do with these driving emotions, these urges? How to animate them into friendship and teacher? "Longing" is the descriptive that seems most supportive. Inspiring in its leaning toward, but also less overwhelming than "craving," more intimate than "desire," and somehow more willing to become ally rather than foe. Longing, a sacred teacher.

In his book *The Return of the Feminine and the World Soul*, Sufi teacher Llewellyn Vaughan-Lee explains, "The heartsickness of the lover is a longing to return to the source in which everything is embraced in its wholeness ... If we can create a context of longing then those whose hearts are burdened with this quest will come to know the true nature of their pain. They will no longer need to repress it, fearing it is as a depression or a psychological problem ... Longing is the pain of separation and at the same time the affirmation of union. It is the dynamic imprint upon consciousness of the soul's memory of the eternal moment when we are together with god. Each moment of longing reminds us of our real nature, and the more potent this pain is the more this memory is alive within the heart. Thus the work of a mystic is to keep this fire burning within the heart, and through devotion and aspiration to let it burn so strongly that it burns away the veils of separation. Then the memory of union becomes a living reality within the heart of the lover. In the fire and pain of this longing the imprisoning walls of the ego gradually dissolve until the eternal moment of the Self can be lived in full consciousness. The Beloved becomes no longer just a hint hidden within the heart, but a constant Companion and Friend ... Longing is the golden thread of the heart's desire."

In some of my late adolescence poems I attempted to write to The Dark One*, for me an imaginary Celtic warrior-lover who, living interiorly in me, rode forth as my first rival and first seducer. Then I knew nothing of Gawain's battle with The Green Knight—the Celtic manifestation of Khidr—nor of his importance to the male seeker. Nor of Khidr himself, the mysterious guide and immortal saint in Islamic lore and Sufic traditions; the hidden initiator of those who walk the mystical path.

The summer of my fifth year I was already catapulting and frolicking myself to a future adult upheaval. I spent all summer in a bright orange dress, emblazoned with giant yellow and red flowers, that had belonged to my adored great aunt Etta. It was if I had stepped from some ancient Indian village, channeling Mirabai. I knew nothing then of Bhakti and other ancient Asian traditions of erotic poetry, of the Troubadours, of Rumi or Tagore, Millay or Akhmatova. My first intuitions of Divine Romance or Devotional Eroticism came, instead, from my elementary and junior high readings of Yeats' thwarted love for Maud Gonne, in the prayerful adorations of *The Song of Songs* and St. John of the Cross, the beguiling romance in fairy and folk tales, and the range of raucous exploits and soulful affections of Greek myth. Tributaries of reading through Yeats and Greek myth guided me to tales of Chivalry and the fantastic in Celtic mythology, Scott, the Romantics, the Pre-Raphaelites, Lewis Carroll, and Lord Dunsany. But I also discovered the impulse in Christian hymnology, such as in the hymn *In the Garden* (Charles A. Miles, 1913) that we sang in the country Methodist church I attended through late adolescence.** I sang the song aloud in my secret hiding place in the top of a mimosa tree in my back yard.

I had, like so many in the 1960s, read Kahlil Gibran and Whitman in elementary school and junior high. In high school, as I began confronting, accepting, and defining my Queer self, I also encountered the more mystical depths of the King Arthur and Grail cycle, and also began reading Lawrence, Rossetti, Hardy, Catullus, Rimbaud, Wilde, Henry Miller, Genet, and Ginsberg. Their scrutiny of love, desire, lust, the body, and spirit seized my imagination. My poems began to take on a much earthier scent, wafting aromas of the Decadents and Symbolists. Personal and artistic equilibrium became imperative lest I drown.

Later still, in college, reading writers such as Rumi (and his beloved Shams), Garcia Lorca, Tagore, Rilke, Kabir, Mirabai, the poem/songs of the Troubadour tradition, my poetic ground became fertile with romantically hypnotic impulses and feelings. Here is when Jung, Sappho, Nin, Rich, Yourcenar, Millay, Plath, and Graves' White Goddess modernized and enlarged my understanding of the myths of love and self-actualization. I took on the assertion that these longings were a karmic gift, and that the archetypes Warrior/Lover, Green Man, Bhaktic Dark One, and Troubadour united in me as poet and Seeker.

My early poems such as *Antinous in Egypt* (in *The Fountain*), the chapbook sequence *Midwinter Fires*, and "middle period" poems *The Green Man's Man**** (in *Gospel Earth*), the cycles *Washing Linen in the River*, *Von Gloeden*, and *Gilgamesh/Enkidu*, evoke in some sense or another Khidr's power and revelation (all of these poems also re-published or published for the first time in *The New Beautiful Tendons*).

Khidr lives and guides those perplexed in the journey—he resides within—and yet can appear in the flesh to walk next to you. Befitting the Green Man, whose footprints leave a green imprint, my poems root themselves in the natural world, the vegetal world.

How will you know the difficulties of being human
if you're always flying off to blue perfection?
Where will you plant your grief-seeds?

We need ground to scrape and hoe,
not the sky of unspecified desire.

What sort of person says that he or she wants to be polished and pure,
then complains about being handled roughly?

—Jelalu'ddin Rumi

The poems in *Verdant* aren't just examples of an intriguing interest in a particular poetic trope; they rose from living experience. In 1995, at the age of forty-two in my mid-life opportunity, as I prefer to characterize it, I fell in love with a younger man, at the expense of my then fifteen-year relationship. That's a long story, not worth telling here, but it was that calamity of spirit and body that made me realize how longing had entrenched itself in me, to my detriment.

Recounting a mythic journey into the transformative energies of grief and longing, in these poems the tenderness and ecstasies and dangerous terrors of my young lover and the affair have been sometimes flattened and sometimes exaggerated. Yes, he was inevitably arrestingly handsome and irresistible—charming and never dull in many sympathetic ways. Those joys and that splendor can be found among the love poems written to the four great loves of my life in *The New Beautiful Tendons: Collected Queer Poems 1969-2012*. As an old and beautiful soul, he too was thrown into a maelstrom of spiritual test. As was my then equally old and beautiful soul-mate (now husband) Stanley (our 42st year in 2022). I portray in these poems a somewhat abstracted imaginal ideal, a vein of encounter, no less true, but not the unabridged story of my generative loves.

A number of synchronic events at the time pointed me to a path of self-discovery, healing, and a return home to Stanley. [How telling that I protested over and over again to my therapist, to Stanley, to our friends that "I would never return *home*."]

Spiritual influences included Ganesha (the Hindu God of Beginnings, patron of letters and sciences, Deva of intellect and wisdom, the great remover of obstacles); a Parsi-born Vedic teacher (eastern and western philosophy professor and follower of Sri Aurobindo, Jehangir Nasserwanji Chubb), and the figure of John

43

the Baptist who, to me, represents the opening of channels between the higher and lower worlds.

I also immersed myself in Akhmatova's and St. Vincent Millay's love poems during this time, absorbing their embodiment of desire and longing deeply knitted in grief, curious as to how their feminine energy wrestled with, overcame, and even dominated their pain and loss, and the terrible and wonderful spell of the Beloved. Their vivid sensations balanced and tempered the more abstracted sanctity of my continued hungry readings in Whitman, Rilke, and Rumi, St. John of the Cross, James Broughton to whom my mentor Jonathan Williams had introduced me, the newly published work *Care of the Soul* by Thomas Moore, and my pre-teen and adolescent friend and guide Gibran.

At my lowest impassioned moment, an unmistakable breakdown, Doris Lessing published her fiercely probing and clarifying novel, *Love, Again* which tells the story of a 65-year-old woman playwright who falls in love with a seductive young actor and then with a more mature, thirty-five-year-old director:

She was raging with desire. (Rage: a good word, like burn) But why describe it, since there is no one who has not felt the mix of anguish, incredulity, and—at the height of the illness—a sick sweet submersion in pain because it is inconceivable that anything so terribly desired cannot be given, and if you relinquish the pain, then the hope of bliss is abandoned too. [...] What was it all about? One falls in love with one's own young self—yes, that was likely: narcissists, all of us, mirror people—but certainly it can have nothing to do with any biological function or need. Then what need? What renewal, what exercise in remembering, is Nature demanding of us? [...] One day the thought had popped whole and fully fledged into her head, as if it had been waiting there for her to recognize it: Am I really to believe that the awful, crushing anguish, the longing so terrible it seems one's heart is being squeezed by cruel fingers—all that is only what a baby feels when it is hungry and wants its mother? [...] It is longing for something just out of its memory; it is longing for where it came from [...] To fall in love is to remember one is an exile, and that is why the sufferer does not want to be cured, even when crying, "I can't endure this non-life, I can't endure this desert." [...]

A strange thing, that when in love or in lust the afflicted ones want most of all to be shut up together in some fastness or solitude, just me and you, only you and me, for at least a year or for twenty, but quite soon, or at any rate after a salutary dose of time, these once so terribly and exclusively desired ones are released into a landscape populated by loving friends and lovers, all bound to each other because they recognize the claims of invisible and secret affinities: if we have loved, or love, the same person, then we must love each other. This improbable state of affairs can only exist in a realm or region removed from ordinary life, like a dream or a legend, a land all smiles. One could almost believe that falling in love was ordained to introduce us to this loving land and its paradise kisses.

The book shattered me. I realized I had come to believe that the Divine Spirit, which I had always thought had protected and guided me, had, instead, abandoned me. Two friends, a mother and her teen-aged daughter, very close friends, came to me that night in pouring rain, to sit with me, hold me, and without judgement, cry with me, allowed my brittle, suffering to be. "Longing for something just out of its memory ... to remember one is an exile."

Mystic philosophers Peter and Maria Kingsley put it this way: "Longing is the movement and the calling of our deepest nature ... if we can find the courage to face it, it will take us back to where we belong ... [It] is the powerhouse of our being ... it breaks everything except what is unbreakable. It shatters all the man-made structures that we try to build up around it and place in its way. It washes away the future and the past and leaves us with nothing but eternity ... time can never contain it ... As we turn away from distractions toward the energy of our longing itself, something extraordinary happens ... What we really want is what has been wanting us since before the beginning of time. Longing longs for us. It wants us to wake up, to become conscious. It is divine intelligence longing to become known. All along we thought it was our longing; assumed that we could do whatever we wanted with it, even run from it if we chose. But how can we run away from our own inner nature, our own divine heritage? We were born to know this mystery."

Three fine women therapists and many wise women friends, in particular, counseled and sometimes chided me. As an afterword to my book *Gospel Earth*, I reprinted the poem "Sorrow, The Awakener"**** by Dr. Chubb, which begins "It is the hand of Love that strikes the blow," and continues, "Then comes great Sorrow with her rude caress / and shakes the sleeper into wakefulness." Dr. Chubb's presence and guidance were instrumental in healing my ravaged self. But without these women's voices defining and demanding I hear and face my longing, my "body hunger" as one of my women friends described it, I would have remained as of air.

Akhmatova, Lessing, and Millay: These became the lodestars of my instinctual confrontation with grief and longing. I began to burn to make a scripture of my exile and return, and thus to evoke personal healing through a sequence of poems rich with the knit of all these poetic expressions and traditions, with all their bitternesses and sweetnesses, while crisscrossing any contemporary idiom with the traditions of the Dark One, Rumi and Shams, Eastern traditions of love songs and laments, and the tender and fragile playfulness of the Radha/Krishna legends. I recalled that little Southern boy in his great aunt's dazzling dress and the young teen who became a young, shy, but sizzling man. I felt no need to revise my gender, but only to remake my image. I pierced my ear and began wearing three silver bracelets as a constant reminder of body, mind, and spirit—of Body, Mind, and Spirit. Without each the corporeal has no wellspring to cool its unreality. Within its inexpressibly luminous dream, Nowhere and Everywhere. Then wakefulness.

As I regained my sanity, as I "came through" as Lawrence would say, I surrendered peaceably to my preoccupation with longing and grief as perennial themes. *Verdant* is one semi-fictionalized result. It took 13 years, or was it 65 (the age at which I completed these), to write these poems, to allow my branch to bend, thirsting and powerless no longer in a Dark Project of my own compellings, but rather one "set on living"? Ezra Pound, in speaking of Dante's art, states, "The tale of Love the revealer, of Love the door and the way into the intelligence, of Love infinite." And in the *Dhammapada* the Buddha instructs:

"Longing gives rise to grief; Longing gives rise to fear. For someone released from longing there is neither grief nor fear."

Ever since I first read W. S. Merwin's translation of Giacomo Leopardi's "L'infinito" I have felt it centered in my heart, mind, and soul, as a brilliant and poignant description of what I was, am still, am always and forever, seeking. Lessing's "invisible and secret affinities."

The Infinite

I ALWAYS loved this hill by itself
and this line of bushes that hides
so much of the farthest horizon from sight.
But sitting looking out I imagine spaces
beyond this one, each without end,
and silences more than human, and a stillness
under it all, until my heart is drawn
to the edge of fear. And when the wind
rustles through the undergrowth near me
endlessly I compare its voice
with the infinite silence. I remember eternity
and the ages dead, and the present,
alive, and the sound of it. So in this
immensity my thinking drowns,
and sinking is sweet to me in this sea.

Giacomo Leopardi

As I began a revision of this book to prepare for print publication, Coleman Barks published his new affecting versions of Rabindranath Tagore's *Gitanjali (Song Offerings)*. When I read # 13 "I have not sung the song I came here to sing," appearing as a preface to this book, and # 96 "When I go from hence let this be my parting word," which closes now this discourse, the unmistakable recognition of their messages floored me. I knew Khidr, the Green Man, the Dark One, the Baptist, stood beside me, one arm wrapped round my shoulder, one hand in my hand, "annihilating," as Andrew Marvel writes, "all that's made / To a green thought in a green shade."

Jeffery Beam
Golgonooza at Frog Level
Hillsborough, North Carolina
Valentine's Day, 2018
Revised Valentine's Day, 2021

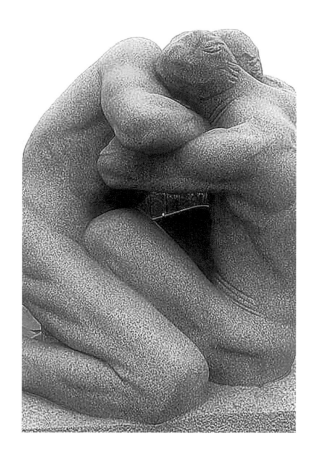

 # 96 Gitanjali (Song Offerings)

WHEN I GO from hence let this be my parting word
—I saw the unsurpassable.

I tasted the lotus' hidden honey
expanding on the ocean of light—

I am blessed—let this be my parting word.

Playhouse of infinite forms!
I played my many parts catching
sight of the formless One.

My whole body and my limbs thrilled
to the touch beyond touch—

If the end comes, let it come—
let this be my parting word.

Rabindranath Tagore

Notes

*In Mirabai's ecstatic poems to Krishna, she lovingly calls him "The Dark One."

**The congregation sang "In the Garden" during the Episcopal Blessing Service of my marriage to Stanley Finch in 2015 at the church he attends, the Chapel of the Cross in Chapel Hill, North Carolina. A civil ceremony, which I had compiled from Christian, Jewish, and texts from Rilke, Kabir, and Shams-I Tabrizi, had taken place a few months before at a friend's house, with ten friends.

***"A Green Narrative in a Green Shade," commentary to the poem "The Green Man's Man," from *Gospel Earth* by Jeffery Beam, Skysill Press, England, 2010:

> Dylan Thomas' "Force that drives the green fuse that drives the flower" alludes, at least in part, to the primal energy signified by the Green Man. Thomas portrays the force's potent urgency toward deterioration and death, but the Green Man's energy, even then, despite Thomas's depressive assessment, brims with fecundity. A figure of unlimited vegetative force, the Green Man appears in many cultures and in many disguises. He survives as both pagan god and Christian icon. In the greater archetypes he is the dying and reviving god of ancient religions, and the Sacred Tree as depicted in the Vedas and in Norse mythology. One can catch a glimpse of him, not yet quite overcome by green, in Neolithic imagery, in Tammuz of the Babylonians, in the Egyptian god Osiris, in the Dionysian Mysteries, and in (*Kur-noo-nohs*) Cernunnos of the Celts. We also sense him in the divinities of Jainism, the American Indian, the Brazilian forest, and in the Aztec God Xipe Tótec (whose "heart is emerald"). He lives in the tales of Robin Hood, Jack-in-the-Green, the King of May, and *Sir Gawain and The Green Knight*.
>
> The Green Man's fertile residence within Christian iconography concentrates, as in no other mythology or religion, in the figure's head. In the West, the oldest type manifests as a single leaf or many leaves forming a male head. In another, vegetation disgorges from his mouth, and even sometimes from his ears and eyes—forming

his hair, beard, eyebrows, and moustache. Finally, in some, his face materializes as fruit or flower born and nestled within the green. His eyes always look at us from the original spring.

For me, the Green Man lives most in the Sufi being, Khidr (a *wali*, or enlightened one, sometime called a prophet or even an angel), known as the Verdant or Green One, whose footsteps leave a green imprint. He appears unexpectedly to the true aspirant and inspired poets when they least expect him and most need him. Khidr, in my opinion, is in all probability the strongest influence on our most familiar church images of the Green Man. After the conquest in the West, Arabic masons and carvers shared not only their highly evolved technical skills, but also their stories, with Romanesque and Gothic artists. Present before then in western culture, the Green Man, at this point, solidifies his power as Christian icon. As a symbol of resurrection and regeneration his image becomes integral, especially from the 11th to the 16th centuries, to many of the great cathedrals and wayside churches of Europe.

The Green Man is not separate from us; he is our source, emphasizing and celebrating the positive creative laws of Nature, the native intelligence that shepherds and protects this world, and the ecological rightness that guides us. The Green Man reveals and bestows life's mysteries—indeed, he embodies them—generating in us the impulse to personify anything that deeply moves us, and compelling us to plow our hands into the soil where his promise dwells, nestled in Persephone's arms, perpetually ready to germinate in and nurture the world.

****For Chubb's poem, "Sorrow, the Awakener" see my book, *Gospel Earth*, (Nottingham, UK: Skysill Press, 2010), page 222. ISBN 978-1-907489-01-3.

"Love's unrelenting seizure" Tamil poet, Manikkavacakar, translated by A.K. Ramanujam.

"I drank to quiet my sorrow" From an anonymous Tartar song, translated by W. S. Merwin.

"The joy counts" Agnes Martin, *Writings/Schriften.*

Rumi, translated by Coleman Barks.

Akmahtova, translated by Judith Hemschemeyer.

Rilke, translated by Babette Deutsch.

Rabindranath Tagore, translated by Tony K. Stewart and Chase Twichell.

Mirabai, translated by David Ladinsky.

Llewellyn Vaughan-Lee, *The Return of the Feminine and the World Soul* (Inverness, CA: Golden Sufi Center, 2009), 194-195.

Doris Lessing, *Love, Again* (New York: Harper Collins, 1996).

Peter and Maria Kingsley, "As Far as Longing Can Reach," *Parabola* 31, no. 2 (Summer 2006): 58-59.

"Longing gives rise" *The Dhammapada,* translated by Gil Fronsdal.

"How peaceful the porch swing" appears as the song "Porch Song Two" in the "chamber opera song cycle" *Family Secrets: Kith and Kin,* by composer Daniel Thomas Davis which premiered with North Carolina Opera and the commissioning soprano Andrea Edith Moore in February 2018, Raleigh, North Carolina. Recording available from Albany Records, www.albanyrecords.com, order no. TROY 1841.

"I am thankful" appeared in *Nimrod International Journal*'s special issue *Mirrors and Prisms: Writers of Marginalized Orientations & Gender Identities,* Spring/Summer 2016, Vol. 59, no. 2. It was also displayed in store windows and on buses in Winston-Salem, North Carolina as part of its 2016 *Poetry in Plain Sight* series of poem posters.

Branch bending in the dew

Photo Credits

Cover photo: Gustav Vigeland sculptural group, Frogner Park, Oslo, Norway. Photo by Paul Lansberg, LPSPhoto ©2013, adapted and used with permission of the photographer.
pf6.lpsphoto.us/130823/094828.jpg

Barberini Faun: Unknown, c. 220 B.C.E., Glyptothek, Munich, Photo Bibi Saint-Pol, 2007. Creative Commons Attribution-Share Alike 3.0 Unported license.

All other photos ©2018, Jeffery Beam.

"Two Fighting Men": Gustav Vigeland sculptural group, Frogner Park, Oslo, Norway.

"Longing: The Dark One's Residence in the Beloved": Philadelphia Museum of Art.

"Man Lifts a Dying Man": Gustav Vigeland sculptural group, Frogner Park, Oslo, Norway.

"Branch bending in the dew": Detail from painter James McGarrell's dining room wall murals "Redwing," Newbury, VT.

Jeffery Beam's over twenty award-winning works include *The Broken Flower, Gospel Earth, Visions of Dame Kind, An Elizabethan Bestiary: Retold* (with artist Ippy Patterson), *The New Beautiful Tendons: Collected Queer Poems 1969–2012,* and *The Fountain.* His spoken word CD with multimedia *What We Have Lost: New and Selected Poems 1977-2001* was a 2003 Audio Publishers Award finalist. *Jonathan Williams: Lord of Orchards* a book of essays, images, and shouts about Beam's mentor, poet and founder of The Jargon Society press, was published in late 2017. The song cycle, *Life of the Bee* (composer Lee Hobby) continues to be performed on the international stage. The Carnegie Hall premiere with the songs and a Beam reading can be heard on Albany Record's *New Growth.*

Composer Steven Sera premiered the cantata *Heaven's Birds: Lament and Song,* using three poems from *The Tendons,* on Boston's World AIDS Day 2008. His tone poem, "An Invocation," inspired by the introductory poem in Beam's book *Gospel Earth,* premiered in 2016 with the Austin Symphony. In July 2016, Serpa premiered in Austin a song cycle, *The Creatures: A Bestiary Retold,* based on eight poems from Beam's *Bestiary* book. Holt McCarley premiered (2015) an instrumental piece, "The Hyena," in St. Louis from the *Bestiary.* 2015 saw the UNC-Chapel Hill premier of *Family Secrets,* a Daniel Thomas Davis song cycle commissioned by soprano Andrea Edith Moore, with Beam's "Porch Song," and texts by other North Carolina authors Allan Gurganus, Randall Kenan, Frances Mayes, Michael Malone, Lee Smith, and Daniel Wallace. North Carolina Opera premiered a re-staging of this work in 2018. A CD recording is now available through Albany Records. Composer Tony Solitro continues to compose works based on Beam's poems. Up to now they are: "Love's Astronomy" for voice and piano (2018) from *The New Beautiful Tendons* which appears on Michelle Murray Fiertek and Michael Korman's CD *Every Tiny Thing* (2012) from Albany Records; "sharp horizons—gentle plains" for clarinet, violin, & piano (2019), inspired by the poem "Earth Gospel" in *Gospel Earth*; and "A Stone Falling, A Falling Stone," for soprano and piano, from the book *The Broken Flower* which premiered in 2020 as part of the American Opera Project First Glimpse. Composer Frank E. Warren is currently working on a number of projects including two song cycles: *The Poppy Suite* and *A Garden of Flowers*. In 2023, Andrea Edith Moore will present, in celebration of Beam's 70th birthday, a concert program featuring selections from the many musical works inspired by Beam's poems, as well as some of Beam's own musical creations.

Kin Press published Beam's last book, *Spectral Pegasus / Dark Movements*, a poetry/painting collaboration, with Welsh painter Clive Hicks-Jenkins. An accompanying CD recording of the poems, including Beam's new "antique" ballad, "Pale Horse," performed with folk-singer Mary Rocap, is available upon request from the author.

On-going projects include two illustrated children's books *The Droods* and a collection of winter lullabies; *A Traveller of Thee: A Poet's Commonplace Book of Poetry and the Spirit*; as well as an anthology of bee poetry, folklore and science throughout time, *Bee, I'm Expecting You*. Beam is poetry editor emeritus of the print and online literary journal *Oyster Boy Review*. He lives at Golgonooza at Frog Level, Hillsborough, North Carolina with his husband of 42 years, Stanley Finch. He retired in late 2011 from many decades as a UNC-Chapel Hill botanical librarian. You can learn more about Beam, and read and hear more of his poetry at his website: jefferybeam.com

ALSO BY JEFFERY BEAM

THE GOLDEN LEGEND (FLOATING ISLAND PUBLICATIONS)

TWO PRELUDES FOR THE BEAUTIFUL (UNIVERSAL)

MIDWINTER FIRES (FRENCH BROAD PRESS)

THE FOUNTAIN (NC WESLEYAN COLLEGE PRESS)

SUBMERGENCES (OFF THE CUFF BOOKS)

LIGHT AND SHADOW: THE PHOTOGRAPHS OF CLAIRE YAFFA
(APERTURE)

VISIONS OF DAME KIND (THE JARGON SOCIETY)

AN ELIZABETHAN BESTIARY: RETOLD (HORSE AND BUGGY PRESS)
(WITH ARTIST IPPY PATTERSON AND PHOTOGRAPHER M.J. SHARP)

LITTLE (GREEN FINCH PRESS)

WHAT WE HAVE LOST: NEW AND SELECTED POEMS 1977-2001
(GREEN FINCH PRESS) (A SPOKEN WORD/MULTIMEDIA 2 CD
COLLECTION)

NEW GROWTH: SHAUNA HOLIMAN AND FRIENDS: NEW SONGS AND
SPOKEN POEMS (CD COLLECTION INCLUDING HOIBY/BEAM'S LIFE OF
THE BEE SPOKEN AND SUNG)

ON HOUNDED GROUND: HOME AND THE CREATIVE LIFE (BOOKGIRL
PRESS, JAPAN) (LIMITED EDITION)

A HORNET'S NEST (THE JARGON SOCIETY/GREEN FINCH PRESS)
(COMPILER/EDITOR—A JONATHAN WILLIAMS MEMORIAL SERVICE
QUOTE BOOK)

AN INVOCATION (COUNTRY VALLEY PRESS) (LIMITED EDITION HAND SEWN FINE PRESS CHAPBOOK)

GOSPEL EARTH (SKYSILL PRESS)

MOUNTSEAEDEN (CHESTER CREEK PRESS) (LETTERPRESS HANDMADE LIMITED EDITION)

MIDWINTER FIRES (SEVEN KITCHENS PRESS REBOUND SERIES) (REPRINT EDITION WITH A NEW INTRODUCTION BY JOE DONAHUE)

THE NEW BEAUTIFUL TENDONS: COLLECTED QUEER POEMS 1969– 2012 (SPUYTEN DUYVIL)

THE BROKEN FLOWER (SKYSILL PRESS)

SACRED SPACES: THE HOME OF ANNE SPENCER (BLURB) (WITH PHOTOGRAPHER JOHN M. HALL)

JONATHAN WILLIAMS: THE LORD OF ORCHARDS (PROSPECTA PRESS) (CO-EDITOR WITH RICHARD OWENS)

*SPECTRAL PEGASUS/ DARK MOVEMENTS (*KIN PRESS) (A COLLABORATION WITH WELSH PAINTER CLIVE HICKS-JENKINS)

COMPOSER'S PRINTED MUSIC FOR WORKS CREATED FROM POEMS CAN BE OBTAINED FROM MANY CLASSICAL VOICE AND INSTRUMENTAL PUBLISHERS, AND/OR DIRECTLY FROM THE COMPOSER'S WEBSITES.

Verdant

Published by Kin Press
Design by J. C. Mlozanowski and Jeffery Beam
Layout and editing by J. C. Mlozanowski

This book was built using Adobe Creative Cloud.
Title pages are rendered in Papyrus, a typeface designed by
illustrator and graphic designer Chris Costello, and inspired by his
study of the Bible. While imagining the writing aesthetic of that era,
Costello developed this typeface by drawing on textured paper with
a calligraphy pen. Poems and essays are presented in Garamond, an
old-style serif font named after the 16th century Parisian engraver
Claude Garamond. Early versions of this typeface were modeled
after the work of punchcutter Francesco Griffo for Venetian printer
Aldus Manutius. This modern version is a revival of the work of 17th
century French punchcutter Jean Jannon.

CPSIA information can be obtained
at www.ICGtesting.com
Printed in the USA
BVHW060123070222
628025BV00001BA/1